The Gorilla in the Room

A Book for Explaining Mental Illness and Stigma to Young Children

By B. L. Acker

Dedicated to my children and my angel Martin, who are the light of my life, my strength to keep going and my inspiration in striving for a healthier life.

A quick note from the author:

I originally contemplated a variety of illustration
for this book but ultimately decided against it.
This is not a storybook intended to be read for fu
at bedtime, full of cute puppies and kittens
frolicking around.

This book is intended to be a stepping stone fo
discussing the very hard topic of mental illness
with children. I believe any illustrations I may
have used would have taken away from the
impact of the words and distracted from the
intent of the conversation.

Whether you use this book in its entirety or as a
template for creating your own conversation, I
sincerely thank you for taking the time to addre.
this topic openly with your children in a healthy
way. I hope that, by talking to our children,
together we can begin to remove the stigma
attached to mental illness.

Everyone gets sick sometimes.

Sometimes, people get sick because they are exposed to viruses or germs.

They might catch something like a cold or the flu. When you can catch an illness from someone else because of germs or viruses, that illness is something called contagious.

And sometimes people become ill because a part of their body isn't working correctly.

There are a lot of illnesses that aren't contagious. You can't catch them from bein near someone who is sick. They occur because a part of someone's body isn't working like it should be working.

Diabetes, for example, occurs when an orga in your body called the pancreas is no longe able to break down sugar in the body like i should. You can't catch diabetes from bein near someone who has it.

Mental Illnesses happen when something isn't working correctly in someone's brain. Mental illness isn't contagious, either.

There are many mental illnesses. They each affect a person's brain in different ways and each have a different name.

Some mental illnesses affect a person's moods, others affect how a person reacts to things that are going on around them. There are others that affect how a person sees the world around them.

No matter what their differences, the one common link they share is that they all occur in the brain.

That is why they are called mental illnesses

Having a mental illness doesn't mean that someone is crazy or that they aren't smart.

It just means that something in their brain isn't working like it should be working.

Mental illnesses can be caused by different things.

Sometimes they are genetic, meaning they are passed from parents to their children much like a child could have blue eyes like their mother or curly hair like their father. When something is genetic, a person is born with it.

A parent having a mental illness doesn't mean a child will definitely have one when they are born, too, though. It sometimes happens but not always.

Other times, mental illness can happen because some very bad things happen in a person's life and their brain doesn't know how to deal with it all.

Sometimes mental illnesses occur because the brain isn't getting everything it needs t work correctly.

No matter what the cause, the reason they are called mental illnesses is because they a start in the brain.

The brain is like a big computer that controls the body, telling it what to do.

It stores memories and helps think up new ideas, too.

It also controls the emotions people feel.

So when the brain isn't working correctly, it not only can affect a person's moods but other things in their body, too.

Because the brain does so many things, doctors and scientists are still studying it an learning how it all works, trying to understand how and why things sometime don't work like they should.

Because doctors and scientists are still learning themselves and don't have all the answers yet to help teach others, there are lot of people who don't understand menta illnesses.

Sometimes people are afraid of things they don't understand.

There are many people who are afraid of mental illness because they don't understand it.

There are other people who are afraid of mental illness because they have heard things about it from other people that, even though they weren't true, it sounded scary to them.

Because those people are scared of mental illness, they sometimes become scared of people that have a mental illness, too.

Sometimes when people are scared of something, they believe it must be bad because it makes them scared.

It is like when a child thinks there is something in their closet or under their bed when they go to bed at night.

Because they cannot see it and don't know what it is, they imagine it must be a big, scary monster.

Sometimes people are scared of what they don't understand.

When people are scared or unsure what to think, their minds usually start to worry bout it being something bad or scary even if it isn't.

Being scared or not understanding something doesn't mean it is bad. Fear might make you imagine something bad, but being afraid of something you don't understand doesn't make those fears real or true. Imagining a monster might be in your closet doesn't mean one is there.

Having a mental illness doesn't make someone a bad person. It just means that something in their brain isn't working like it should right now.

Sometimes people become scared of peop
with mental illness because they have hear
exaggerated stories about it either from
other people they know or from movies o
television.

An exaggeration is when someone makes
something seem much bigger than it really
like saying you have hundreds of apples
because it seems like you have too many t
count, when you really only have twenty.
just seems like a lot more.

When someone exaggerates about menta
illness, it can make it seem a lot scarier tha
it really is.

Sometimes people have heard that someone who had a mental illness did something bad so they assume everyone who has a mental illness must be bad, too. That is called a generalization.

That would be like thinking that everyone with blue eyes was mean because one person with blue eyes was mean to you.

It wouldn't fair to all the people with blue eyes who haven't done anything wrong.

Just like it isn't fair to generalize that everyone with a mental illness is bad because a few people with mental illness did something wrong.

Sometimes people believe things that aren' true just because it was something that people used to believe was true years ago, before they learned the truth.

Many years ago, people used to believe many things that seem silly today.

For example, people used to believe that th earth was flat before scientists discovered i was round.

eople also used to believe all types of things bout mental illness that we've since learned aren't true.

Many people used to believe that having a mental illness made someone evil, dangerous or many other negative things.

Sadly, even though doctors and scientists have proven that none of it is true, some people still believe it just because others used to believe it was true.

All of those feelings and opinions that people believe even though they aren't true are all examples of stigma.

Stigma is when people attach negative feelings and beliefs to something or someone, whether it is based on generalizations, exaggerations or things that are not true that some people still believe anyway.

Mental illness has a lot of stigma because so many people don't understand it and people sometimes think bad things about things they don't understand.

When people don't understand something or it scares them, many people don't want to talk about it.

They pretend it isn't there or that it isn't important enough to talk about because it makes them uncomfortable to admit that it scares them or that they don't understand it.

But ignoring something or pretending it isn't there doesn't make it go away.

Millions of people in the world today have some type of mental illness.

That is not an exaggeration.

Because so many people in the world have mental illness, it might seem silly that som people are trying to ignore it and pretend i doesn't exist.

It would be like having a giant gorilla sittin in the middle of your kitchen while everyor ate dinner and your family pretending the didn't see him.

It is very silly to ignore something so big tha everyone knows is there.

Yet many people still pretend mental illness isn't there or isn't important because it is hard for them to talk about it, whether it makes them scared or they just don't understand it.

Mental illness is like that giant gorilla sitting there at your kitchen table.

It won't go away just because some people pretend it isn't there.

You don't have to pretend it isn't there. It is okay to talk about it and to ask questions.

The only way for a person with a mental illness to get better is for them to get treatment for their illness.

Sometimes that means going to a doctor to talk about what caused their mental illness and to get treatment.

Sometimes it means taking medicine that helps give a person's brain what it needs so it can work properly again.

Sometimes a doctor will recommend other treatments that might help them feel better and make their mind stronger again.

Though doctors and scientists are still learning about the brain, they have developed ways to treat different mental Ilnesses that make life better for the people with them.

Sometimes, with treatment, mental illnesses can fade so much that they seem to almost go away completely.

Other times, the mental illness is not as easy to treat. Some mental illnesses will always be there and will always need treatment, though with treatment, things won't be as bad.

It might seem scary to you that they are going to the doctor or that they need to tak medicine.

But it is nothing to be scared about. They just have an illness and are seeing a docto so that they can get better.

It just might take a little time for their doctors to find the treatment that works best for them because everyone is differen

When someone has a mental illness, what they really need from everyone around them is patience and understanding.

Sadly, many people with mental illness have had to deal with judgments and stigma from other people who don't understand mental illness or who are scared of it.

Stigma and judgments like that are not fair.

Stigma and judgments are not fair because nobody asks to be sick or to have a mental illness.

Mental illnesses can happen to anyone.

Having a mental illness doesn't make you a bad person any more than having any other illness would make someone a bad person.

It just means something in that person's brain is not working like it should right now.

t is important to treat someone with mental
Ilness fairly because they are people just like
everyone else.

They just happen to have an illness affecting
their brain right now.

But they are still people. And they have
done nothing wrong to deserve being
treated badly. They are not scary.

They are just ill right now.

Mental illness doesn't discriminate.

That means it doesn't matter whether you are a boy or girl, how old you are, what color your skin is, where you come from, what religion you practice, who you love, or how much money you have.

Mental illness affects many different people from all over the world.

It doesn't matter who they are. Anyone can have a mental illness.

Mental illness isn't contagious.

You can't catch a mental illness from being around somebody who has one.

You shouldn't avoid someone just because they have a mental illness.

Their mental illness won't rub off on you and make you sick, too.

A person who has mental illness is not evil dangerous or scary just because they are il

Though there might be stories about a few people with a mental illness who did something wrong, that is only a few people out of millions of people.

You should never generalize that everyone with a mental illness is bad because a few people with a mental illness did something wrong.

You should never let the opinions of other people based on stigma or fear make you treat someone with mental illness any differently.

Ignoring mental illness or pretending it isn't important is just as silly as trying to ignore a gorilla at your dinner table.

There are a lot of people who don't understand mental illness, but is nothing for you to be scared about.

It is okay to talk about mental illness and ask questions. It is just another illness that people can have that needs to be treated so they can get better.

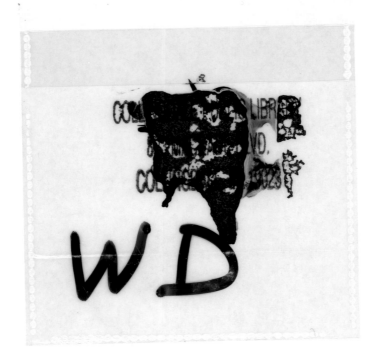

WD

CPSIA information can be obtained
at www.ICGtesting.com
Printed in the USA
BVHW04s2146100718
521358BV00009B/81/P

9 781979 658485